I0553120

Conchas y Café Zine
Vol. VII, Issue 2

Caring for the World

a  publication

DSTL Arts presents

Caring for the World

Conchas y Café Zine
Vol. VII, Issue 2

Cover and Book Design: Luis Antonio Pichardo

ISBN: 978-1-946081-59-9

10 9 8 7 6 5 4 3 2 1

www.DSTLArts.org

Los Angeles, CA

Table of Contents

That Seed

Mojdeh Amini

As a child was planting wildflower seeds ambitiously
swallowed a seed adventurously

That seed seated somewhere inside me soundlessly
started drinking and dining in my body vigorously

As a child felt it's rooting in my heart chords, cancerously
skipped my beats slowly but catching them fast and furiously

That seed surrounded my backbone and climbed to my brain
    dangerously
Sealed my orders to myself and turning them into codes to fool
    me suspiciously

As a child went to the brain mapping center, to snapshot it
    asperously
spread to my brain and hairs continuously
like a bunch of whirlwinds, wildflowers were blooming at a top
    of a tree generously

how to pet a rabbit

Ayan Ortega

be careful not to break
their thin bones

16 vertebrae in the tail
longer than the cartoons
make them out to be

it may wrap around
your pinky finger
as you hold them

you can count them
if you run along
each section
and feel each ridge
as it curves

but be careful not to
pinch or twist
their little bones
fragile as they are

to pet a rabbit
you must wait

for them to come to you
do not force them
or they will run off

pounding their hind feet to the ground
as they retreat into
the darkest corner

to pet a rabbit
do not squeeze too tight

they just might
twist in revolt
and break

their own
fragile little spine

You Are Missed

Lois Jackson King

The loving friendship is now gone
The loving friendship shall linger on
The loving friendship that was so aware
The loving friendship showed so much care
The loving friendship is no more to share

All things don't stay the same
All things, like some, carry no blame
All things aren't always sweet; some are lame
All things, somehow, seem not to fit
All things, or many things in life, is the pits

I will never forget your smiling face
I will never forget your warm embrace
I will never forget how you gently wiped my butt
I will never forget how you took care of my small cut
I will never forget, no, I will never forget

I'll always remember your patience with me
I'll always remember being read to because I couldn't see
I'll always remember your voice; a sweet spirit of love
I'll always remember you telling me to stay strong
I'll always remember you singing songs, so I could sing along

They Call Me the Light

Gustavo Reyes Ramirez

Me llamo *Pablo*
But they call me *Luz*.

Dementia.
At first they called me Pablo.
Next they called me son.
Then they called me thief.
Then, a brother.
　…then, a total stranger.

Alzheimer's.
They couldn't remember my name.

Hospice.
Then they forgot who I was entirely.

I am Nurse.
But I call them
All
　　　Familia.

DEMENTIA

Michelle Smith

(D)o I know how to care for

you my belove(D)?

(E)ventually I cannot bear that you won't know m(E).

(M)y God, did genetics

play a role to plague hi(M)?

(E)ncourage me to be

love,

light,

and strength,

for easy the embarking

on this journey will not b(E).

(N)ew ways to teach you,

Will it last longer the(N)?

(T)enacity of a terminal illness as we age, you and I envisioned no(T).

(I)ntelligence you never lacked;

Your taus and plaques synapsed

the memories,

place,

time,

and stimuli(I)

(A)lone I am not,

family

support groups

1.800.FortheALZ is a phone call away.

D E M E N T I A
has seven stages and is not
a melodrama or telenovel(A).

Summer Breeze

Tina Fallon

Summer breeze, I think of you
Summer breeze, I get the blues
Summer Breeze, the song you love
Summer breeze, you watch above

It tears me apart, the melody
It tears me apart, endlessly
It tears me apart, too much sorrow
It tears me apart, the toy piano

On the old street, I'm younger
On the old street, you're stronger
On the old street, you play your guitar
On the old street, camping and race cars

On the old street, we're all together
It tears me apart, the song you love
Summer Breeze, it tears me apart

Restless Souls

Mojdeh Amini

In salute to Ukrainians

For millions in this world,
world is ending right now
when the winter snow is cuddling and kissing naked trees

Trees are pouring down kisses on the unrestful bodies
Bodies of the brave wits are piling up
Up to the shaky smoky sky

Sky askew to grip and grasp the restless souls
Souls are uprising and twinkling the lonely sky
Sky without no stars is flickering lives and echoing songs

Hospice

Katherine Vega

Holding onto the souls in between the worlds, the

Onus now turned to you to translate what is happening

Specializing in the truth of who we are as humans and spiritual
beings

Pleasing grieving family members who aren't ready, but look
for peace

Igniting insight to each minute, each breath, each motion

Championing the love, the faith, and the peace

Everyone is grateful for the extra attention, life force, and wisdom
needed to say goodbye

Cuarto No. 14

Sanjui Martinez

Yacía allí con su corazón entero
Y sin aliento alguno.
Que decían que ya no estaba
Que había cumplido su voluntad.
Noventa inviernos en su rostro lucía.
Las mil líneas en su rostro revelaba
Cuanto tiempo a todos cuido.

Mi abuela, ya no estás.
Te fuiste cuándo lo decidiste.
Ni un centimetro de ti
Mostraba ser motivo de tu partida.
Más bien, fue tu insistencia
De seguirlo a él, mi abuelo.

Ay abuela, ya no estás.
Dejaste un vacío difícil de llenar
Un montón de recuerdos.
Una familia sin timón.
Ya sin ti viene la disolución.

Ay abuela, ya no estas.
Te fuiste con agallas.
Demonstraste que al final

Ibas a irte si querías.

Porque él vendría

ya lo sabias.

Ay abuela, ya no estás.

Vacío dejaste el Cuarto No. 14.

Left My Side

Lois Jackson King

I miss you my dear care provider; you were very kind
I miss your tender way of helping; I never felt neglected
I miss you because of the times of your encouragement
I miss your wonderful attitude and sweet hellos
I miss you just not being here, to give care to me

Your way of caregiving I truly do miss
Your way, the way you brought light into my darkness
Your way, how you helped me to continue to look past my pain
Your way, that to me, a way of new life to breath
Your way, I regret, is now no longer by my side

Remembering the joyful times, you made me feel better
Remembering the way you helped me to dress so I looked my best
Remembering the times you wiped away my many tears
Remembering the many ways you provided extra care
Remembering the kindness of your care, I do really miss

Blessed caregiver, which gave service from the heart
Blessed caregiver, giving medical attending from the start
Blessed caregiver gave me much care, as well as hope
Blessed caregiver, oil me down as to hide my ash
Blessed caregiver, from this life, has blessedly passed

Scatter Me to The Moon

Mojdeh Amini

Hey, me ending soon as melting drop, drop

Operations and pills all went out the windows, ya, ya

Sing and dance me let's confuse and sleep all the pains

Picture me and take me to the wildest seashores

I fly to the sky and sea waves to you and I

Carry me and scatter my ashes with my vociferous red-eyed vireo

End me, when my vireo and the wind whistling to the moon

Experiencias trabajando con la tercera edad

Rocio Diaz

Compartimos tiempo, pero el tiempo de ellos está limitado

Lo veo cuando sus cuerpos regresan a la niñez

Con cariño los atiendo, con el tiempo mi corazón se encariña
con el de ellos

Cuando sus almas dejan sus cuerpos y su ser ya no es, vacío se
queda mi ser

Alejandra, Experiencias Trabajando con Personas de la Tercera Edad

Abraham Jaramillo

A tiempo, a ver que les hago de comer

cenar y tomar

no cualquier cosa

cuerpos cansados

bañarlos es pesado

A tiempo, para sus píldoras y cápsulas

cuerpos frágiles y aveces rendidos,

pero siempre agradecidos

a veces no recuerdan mi nombre

mentes deterioradas

puerta debe permanecer

siempre cerrada

sino se me van

A tiempo, para verlos

un último adiós

no cualquier cosa

no solo cuerpos

personas,

madres, hermanos,

amigos, tíos

A tiempo, a ver que hago de comer
lavar y barrer
no cualquier casa
mi casa
el cuerpo descansa
mientras la tele presenta
una nueva novela.

Alejandra, Experiences Working with the Elderly

Abraham Jaramillo

On time, let's see what I can make them to eat

dine and drink

not just anything

tired bodies

bathing them is heavy work

On time, for your pills and capsules

fragile bodies sometimes surrender,

but always grateful

sometimes they don't remember my name

deteriorated minds

door must remain

always closed

otherwise they would get out

On time to see them

one last goodbye

not anything

not just bodies

people,

mothers, brothers,

friends, uncles

On time, let's see what I make to eat

wash and sweep

not just any house

my home

the body rests

while the TV presents

a new telenovela.

DSTL Arts

Karyn Grasse

Develop, like a polaroid,

Skills we don't even know we possess.

Transcending with a mere thought,

Limits fading from us all.

Abstractions revealing each aura,

Reaching for the elixir

That encapsulates what

So passionately we long to express.

Compassion

Lois Jackson King

Care you gave to me, like none other
Opening to work, a wonderful and sweet caring heart
Many times over you were a comfort to me
Placing me in bed, and whispering you'll be fine
Attending to me with a smile as I was being fed
Sweet and gentle are your ways toward me
Shining a light of joy, in my life, as you worked
Inspiring words of encouragement kept me lifted
On time and in time for every scheduled service
Never mumbling about and duties you performed

In the Field

Jing (Heidi) Wu

I ran in the fields,

The fragrance of the earth is refreshing,

I ran in the fields,

The yellow wildflowers swayed and smiled at me,

I ran in the fields,

The unfolding voice relaxes me,

I ran in the fields,

The heavy rice in autumn bends over like a smile,

I ran in the fields,

It seems to go back to the joyous and

happy days of childhood.

I ran in the fields,

The earth hugs me like a mother listening

to my childlike crying,

I ran in the fields,

The setting sun and the hills on the horizon seem

to merge into one,

I ran in the fields,

The green broad-bean leaves opened like a

mouth and laughed at me,

I ran in the fields,

The chubby baby opened his mouth and smiled at

me as if I could understand the baby's lips,

I ran in the fields,

Two birds flying side by side with beautiful feathers like

a loving couple,

I ran in the fields,

The setting sun seemed to be guiding me home.

Yesterday, Today and Still

Mojdeh Amini

Yesterday, in COVID 20 and 21,
leaders were carrying wines and whiskies
in shopping bags and suitcases carelessly.
Heading to the Down Streets Garden
Gathering, partying and enjoying lives selfishly
Ask Boris and Sue more about it

Today, in COVID 22,
people are carrying guns and Molotov cocktails
in shopping bags and suitcases carefully
with one eye looking up to the sky
Fighting and giving lives sincerely
Ask both Vladimir and Volodymyr,
Putin and Zelensky more about it

Still, in COVID 22,
People are waking up or losing life by cruise missiles
and air strikes through the free air zones and human shields
Offering a "ride" to the Pres. not helping them
Back to sleep, neither life nor meaning of life, seriously!
Ask Joe and Kamala more about it

Untitled Father Poem

Nikolai Garcia

You're gone and
          you left us
Left us with
          unpaid bills
Left us with
          a mortgage payment
Left us with
          Mexican-work-ethic

Father you went away
          too soon
A life gone
          too soon
To the graveyard
          too soon

We miss you
          in our lives
We miss
          your strength
We miss
          your guidance

Left us

Too soon

We miss you

pieces of you

Ani Minasian

you leave a trail
I follow

eggshell fragments
sugar-free candy wrappers
scraps from a Splenda packet

my reassurances
I still have you

just cleaned this floor
don't clean enough

but I have you

don't really care about the floor

Charity

Luz Donis

Called are the

Heedless

And the conscientious.

Repair

Inequalities

That

You witness.

Home of the Braves

Mojdeh Amini

Here is the home of the braves
Here is the home of the remembrance and hope
Here is the home of the well knowns and never be knowns
Here is the home of the forsaken voices and broken pens

Your footsteps are everywhere in our stories and poems
Your footsteps are everywhere in our minds and thoughts
Your footsteps are everywhere in the sky over the bridges
Your footsteps are everywhere in the cemeteries and theaters

You born again when the winter meets the spring
You born again when the swallows sing over the spring branches
You born again when the impossible dreams become possible
You born again when the flag anthem raises our cry of happiness
        and heart beats

Here is the home of the braves
Your footsteps are everywhere in our stories and poems
You born again when the winter meets the spring

To Be or Not

Lois Jackson King

Let me out, I do scream and roar, throughout the day

With my crazy thinking, I feel the fear will soon fade away

Restrained and tortured; self-inflicted, suffering and emotional fear

I will be released from these spiritual snares and be of good cheer

I say I can do it anytime, rather night or during the day

Am I tired of trying so hard; should I go or should I stay

I know all this has been tried many times before

I must be stronger than I am, no more false-hinged doors

Just wait, I'll do it quick and fast, or courage will hit the floor

Maybe a strong prayer, or booster shot, is what I need

The desire of my inner spirit is making this mighty plea

Rambling, scrambling, trying hard to make up my mind

Dear Lion Muse of mine, the inner strength I need to find

Your roaring power is real; telling me you can and you will

A lioness spirited heart is in me; come forth as a fulfilling meal

Forward I will go; no turning back; facing challenges and making
     my stand

No more excuses, to be found; a stronger existence, I am in
     this land

"Roar Roar Roar"; my inner Muse; go ahead and let no one change
     the plan

Removing false shadows of past hurts, rejection, and shame

Realizing the inside fears are gone; I'm truly free from all blame

Remembering, I hold a strong inner strength from which I'll
     never depart

Being that one I know I can be; fearless spirit of power, of a
        Lioness Heart

Listen to the Mockingbird

David Fallon

He sings a song of grief

Of lands lost

Of lost souls

Of souls forgotten

Of forgotten times

His song fills the air

Like a thousand needles

Stinging like an angry hornet

The wail of a horn

Penetrating the air

With sounds of madness

Then he is sweetness and light

A twitter that brings delight

That takes the fighting out of the fight

Like sugar dancing on the tongue

As when spring has sprung

And the cage bird's sung and sung

Listen to the Mockingbird

He knows the world

Better than we know ourselves

He preaches a knowledge

Long buried inside

He wants only to fill the void

To chase away longing and despair

He wants only to bring us closer

To what we are meant to be

Play My Little Sea Otter

Katherine Vega

Knowing you are there sweet little Sea Otter

Ready to dance

Open to play

Prepared to hug

Eager to share

Aligned that you are joyous little Sea Otter

Supporting those that you love

Giving to those you don't know

Feeling unconditional love for everyone you meet

Holding being the mother to the world

Brilliance encompasses you beautiful Sea Otter

Easily Creating genius with your playful spirit

Lovingly gifting the world with your wisdom

Warmly listening to those that need to be listened to

I know that you live inside me.

I can feel you.

You feel me!

Feel me hiding you?

Feel me binding you?

Feel me bringing you to the surface and holding you back
down again?

I hold you down when I hear you and don't listen to you

I hold you down when you want to love someone but I am terrified

I hold you down when I don't pay my bills on time and you want
to be in the flow

I hold you down when I don't
Write

Act

Improvise

Dance

Sing

...........although we both ache to

But......

When I take a shower and allow myself to cry

I ignite that part of us that can love unconditionally

When I sing a song from my heart

I ignite that part of us that can express our creativity

When I bring my budget to balance

I ignite the freedom to swim with the flow and others

When I meditate

I connect to the wisdom of who we are

Thank you for the gift you little sea otter

I will work hard not to hold you down during our lifetime

Writer's Block

Karyn Grasse

I see you there

Blank Page

With your fancy watermark,
And your 24-pound linen weave,
Smugly basking in your 102 brightness.

Staring at me

Laughing at me

Mocking me
With your

      Whiteness

Your

      Blankness

Playing on all my darkest insecurities:

      You have no original thoughts.

You're not even a writer.
You're a FRAUD.

I will not be defeated!

I will reach out
And defile you with

a

Mark!

Ha!

Fall Foliage

Mojdeh Amini

It's fall when falling in love with the beautiful Iowan's reddish, golden yellow, and brownish fall foliage, easily and blindly

I'm walking and running among the deciduous trees with their colorful falling leaves trying to catch them foolishly and fearlessly by the Mississippi River

It's fall when falling in love with exciting California and its colorful Fall foliage when going down to reach and kiss the Los Angeles River

I'm watching and hearing the rivers' waves dancing up and down to reach to the thirsters and the hungers to fill and nourish them

It's fall when falling in love with the funny sky when is raining gray in the morning, shining blue at noon, and laughing red in the afternoon

I'm looking up to the sky and counting and recruiting its stars, one, two, three... to help me find my way through their lights

It's fall when falling in love with its dark insightfully and behind my imagination

I'm keeping my feelings while passing through the dark and the darkest, to hear and echo my thoughts, by asking the stars to shine more generously

I'm calling the past time to find the promising exit from this darkness, its strong gravity might create a novel version of us to survive and to shine

Empty Room

Nikolai Garcia

The television glows. Spongebob is on
the screen annoying his cartoon neighbor
with maniac laughter.

A cat curls up in a corner, content
to be left alone
but wishes someone had fed him.

The bunk beds are unmade. Legos
are half-formed ideas scattered
on the floor waiting to be stepped on.

A Nintendo Switch is plugged into a wall
socket, battery charging. A stack of textbooks
sits quiet, waiting to be acknowledged.

I sit on a bed, smile at the cat,
who now cries for food. All
the while, Spongebob continues to laugh.

Getting Away

Sanjui Martinez

Eyeing it from the corner
To make sure it has not moved.
I know what is needed.
It is just not yet.

So out I go.
To enjoy the day.
The wind.The flowers. The rain.

Back at home it awaits me
To fill it with letters, words, and stories of long ago.
But I turn my back and block it off.
And drive down the many winding streets
As fast or as slow I go
Knowing that no matter how far I go,
No matter how long I go
I will have to return
To that which I promise I love
But maybe not enough.

So the clock ticks.
And the sun has set.
Everyone makes their way home
But me.

Because I know what awaits.

As Midnight checks in,
My mind's delight appears.
Street lights, slow music,
I hear it. I see it. It is there.

My notebook awaits to converse with me.
And the story goes...it is time now.

Full Moon

Ani Minasian

she knows
a full moon is coming

I pull down the blinds
black out the drapes
still she knows

she paces past the windows
she claws at the door and
gnaws on furniture
soon she'll begin to snarl and
growl, her frustration growing
why are the doors barred
why are the windows shuttered
how will she get out

outside the tangled brambles
twist, the warbling
nightingales call
a gale raps
on the walls and roof
slapping tree branches
and hurtling
leaves

her red eyes crack
her fur pulled up and
out in all directions
a full moon
is coming

I can try to keep her locked in
but it's risky
for if I don't let her out
now and then to run
wild in the moonlight and
howl at the stars
I may one day wake
finding her clenched teeth
clamped around my throat
her paws pressed
down upon my chest
cutting off
my air, siphoning
off blood

a full moon is coming
and if I don't soon
set the beast free
you may not like what you see
for she could very
well devour me

whole and next

she'll turn her sights
on you, you wouldn't
like that
would you

The Me and The Sea

Mojdeh Amini

*Writing to **The Old Man and the Sea** by Ernest Hemingway*

Gave me the book for digging

Rooted in the sea of the warrior

Asked all the Marlins in the old man and the sea

None remembered you, searched for an unbridled Marlin

Days after days but added more sharks around me instead

Passed them all, giving a piece of me to each, felt lighter for
digging up

And now pin my remaining pieces into the secrecy of your sea

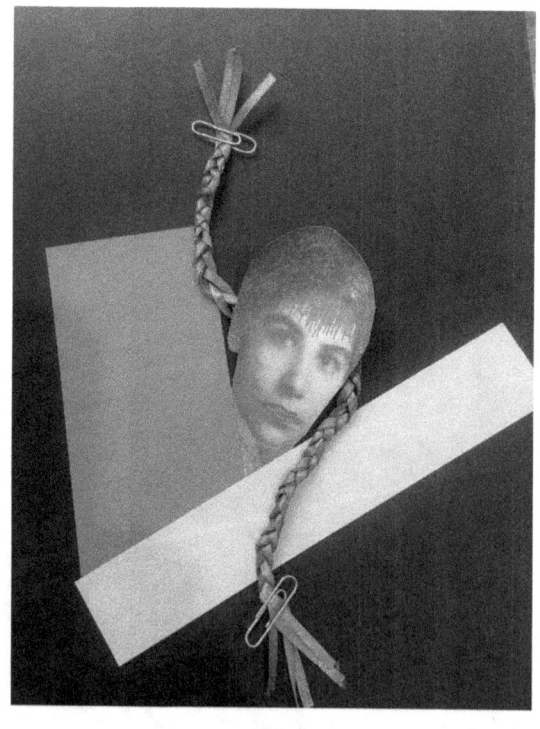

Want to Play

David Fallon

Jenny spread the worksheets onto the kitchen table. She plucked a pencil from the pencil case and noticed that it was covered in bite marks. She frowned and tossed it into the trash. She opened the case again to see that all of the pencils had bite marks. Shaking her head, she dumped them all into the trash before opening the desk drawer to find a brand new one. She stuck it into the sharpener with a low grinding sound. When she was satisfied with its sharpness, she set it next to the worksheets and called out:

"Ok, Ben, it's time!"

There was no response.

"Ben, it's time!" she called again.

Several more seconds went by with no response. Jenny sighed loudly and stood up to walk to the front door. As expected, Ben was standing quietly with his face toward the door. This was what he did when he wanted to avoid doing something, like worksheets.

"Ben–"

"Want to go out," Ben interrupted.

"Ben–"

"Want to go out."

"It's not time to go out," Jenny put her hand on Ben's shoulder. "It's time for worksheets."

"Don't want worksheets," Ben said. "Want to go out."

"Outside is later," Jenny sighed. "First is worksheets. Then lunch. Then TV time. And then maybe outside time later."

"No later," Ben shrugged her hand off of his shoulder. "Want outside time now!" He was starting to get upset.

"Ok," Jenny breathed out slowly. "We'll go outside. But

we have to do the other things first."

Ben stomped his foot hard on the ground. He turned around suddenly and headed for the kitchen. When Jenny followed, she saw that he was already at the table with the new pencil in his mouth.

"No chewing please," Jenny took the pencil from his mouth and handed it to him. He gave that grunt growl sound that she did not like. She stepped away to pour herself some more coffee. She could tell it was going to be a long day.

"Don't want adds and subtracts!" Ben pushed the paper away.

"Come on, Ben," Jenny sat in the chair next to him and brought the paper back."I'll help you."

"Don't want it!" he threw the pencil, and it bounced off the table landing on the floor. Jenny bent over to pick it up.

"I hate it, Jenny!" The sound of her name rang through her ears. It was always jarring to hear him say her name. He almost never said it. Only when he was angry or distressed.

"Want to play!" Ben said with tears in his eyes.

Play was an issue. As a 46-year-old man with the intellect of a 6-year-old, Ben did not really have any friends. He could not play with small children, and there were very few adults like him to hang out with. This meant that most of the time his playmate was Jenny, which was awkward because she was also his caretaker. It was a dynamic that caused endless difficulty in their relationship. Of course, Jenny wanted Ben to have fun and enjoy life. But she also had to make sure he was doing the basics like cleaning himself and doing his worksheets.

"We can't play right now–"

"Don't want it!" Ben pushed everything off the table onto the floor, then got up and bolted to the door where he stood quietly waiting.

Jenny slowly gathered the items and placed them back on the table. She got why he didn't like doing the work. His abilities never really changed. While he could easily add 2+2 as 4, he struggled with 5+5 by inverting the 5s and answering 4 instead of 10. He still wrote his name B3N using a 3 instead of an E.

"Too stupid!" he would yell every time he got them wrong. Every time it broke Jenny's heart. Why did everything have to be so difficult?

Just last week, she was shocked to discover that Ben remembered their mom. For thirty years he never mentioned her. Out of the blue, he asked: "Where's mom?" Jenny burst into tears. Ben never knew their father. He left when Ben was just a year old, not man enough to face his responsibility to his disabled son. Mom he knew until she died of cancer when he was ten years old.

"I'm sorry," their mom whispered to Jenny on her deathbed.

"Don't worry, I'll take care of him," was all Jenny could think of to say.

"Okay," Jenny brushed away a tear and pushed the chair back as she stood. She grabbed her keys and headed to the front door. "Let's go play."

Firefly

Luz Donis

*Para Tia Estela quien
deleitaba en llamarme
"Luciernaga"*

It's summertime
you can come out now
during dusk
from my darkness.

Yes, I put you in that jar
such a very long time ago.
It was just for play
or maybe envy.
I almost forgot you, firefly
thought you were dead.

I've seen you twinkle and flash
your coded signals.
Why do you bother, my flashy friend?
All you ever do
is make me acutely aware
of my discontent.

No, it's not enough to just know you
It's so much easier to cancel you.

With bright colorful pixels
from small and big screens
though unlike them
you never shut off.

Your lumens feed on knowing
emanating the warmth of understanding.
How do you do that?
Who do you think you are?

Go on light your tiny torch
keep trying to awaken me.
Guide me through
a separate reality.

Catch my eye
firefly
with a twinkle and a wink.
When I'm restlessly
sitting in the dark
quietly alone.

Light to the World

Lois Jackson King

You, I care a lot about you, I don't want to be without

My best of friends, until every episode comes to an end

I enjoy your very presence, in the day and in the night

You have the great ability to bring light when I see only the dark

I care for you; seeing you not as an idol, but a friend unmarked

Channeling here, and channeling to there, faithful; always to view

The wonderful relationship which we have is quite a normal one

But so many have yet to have it in place and see life as done

Your ability helps me care; it ushers in new experiences of things

I am so filled with joy when you help me to hear others sing

Many times I have fallen asleep; by my side you are still here

My big, bright 50 inch TV screen; for you I really, really care

Life of Earth

Mojdeh Amini

Wine of life

Oasis of love

Mother of earth

Eagle of peace

Nest of souls

Kusi Wasi

Katherine Vega

Not one

Not two

Not three

or even 10

20

or a million colors

can reflect the vibrancy that I choose to live in

Yellow like the sun shining greets me

Walking through door

Bringing you feelings of joy and light

Prepare for a colorful experience

We will share in both of our lights and joy

Red bring my heart

To the center of my living room

Joining people together to share

To Express love and warmth

Love is the key for us to exchange

Orange expressing the nutrients

That are put together to feed myself and others

Compartiendo that cafecito while bonding

Taste this and feel full of love

Holding the warmth that wraps us in the wonderful embrace

Green to ground us into the earth
Powdering our noses and have a private moment
Anchoring into our bodies
And listening to our needs
A safe space for you to be free and relaxed

Pink to feel creativity
Creating to contribute
Manifesting abundance
Sharing my light to the world
You sharing your light with the world
Together we create magic

Lavender reminding us of serenity
Bringing us a time of rest
Rest for you
Rest for me

Colors Here
Colors Everywhere
I welcome you to Kusi Wasi,
the House of Peace, Harmony, and Joy

Sin Sed

Rocio Diaz

Frutos nacen de mi cuando dejo
que mi alma tome agua, con las caricias
inocentes de mis sobrinos, cuando convivo
con el amigo fiel de los ojos
color miel, cuando mi reflejo
femenino se multiplica, dejo caer
mi vestido rosa y ellas iluminan mi ser

Cuando la madre naturaleza acaricia
las raíces de mis pies, perfumándome
con tranquilidad y purés, llenando mi vacío
con un jardín de gardenias, así
es como vuelvo a florecer, regreso
en carne y hueso para convertirme
en voz, la voz
que cobija y aboga
por los derechos de mi
comunidad indocumentada

Relational Caring

Lois Jackson King

As I think back to the tides of past and gone

Those reminiscing and loving thoughts which linger on

The persons who were once here made me who I am

Where should I start, with the ones which did their part

First, there was mom, who couldn't handle all the things just right

But she did what she could, through ups and downs and a few fights

Then her mom, dear Grandma, with caring arms, saved me many times

Let's not forget mom's grandmother, my great grand, who shared love

Her hands, washing clothes, in a boiling pot; her home now is above

They gave to me what they had to offer; some bad, but more good

I was able to receive the presence of a great, great grandmother

Showing love instead of hate; no matter the color I discovered

Part Indian, and white, black husband; dark children, no running for cover

Caring for all mankind, she did, when all odds were trying to push her down

She gave of herself, but she too is gone, and I never saw her frown

Her loving way of caring was of true love; and color had no ground

Her attitude gave me a positive start; from this, I shall never depart

Mother

Nikolai Garcia

Makes coffee every morning

Of course, she wakes up first

Thinking of others before herself

Helping until it hurts

Everything for her children

Rewards our lives with loving bursts.

Have You Seen My Dad?

Mauricio "Soul on Fire" Moreno

Do you know if he'll be back
to tuck me in at night?
If he'll be there at dawn,
to welcome me into the day?

It's hard to see because
I don't have his eyes. I can't
tell if the lights welcome
me or demand I show my hands.

It's hard to hear because
I don't have his ears. I can't
tell if the sounds are fireworks
or bullets, whether I should

look up or duck down.
It's hard to think because
I don't have his mind. I can't
tell if I should speak or run,

whether my tongue will save
my life or take it away. It's
hard to feel because I don't
have his hands. I can't tell

if, when I reach out, I feel
a warm embrace or iron bars.
It's hard to walk because he's
not here to guide me. Where

is the North Star? If I find it
on my own, will it lead
me out of the South Side?

It's hard to stay quiet because
I don't know his authority. I can't
tell when to speak up or listen,
no tough love to smooth my rough edges.

It's hard to believe because
I don't have his faith. I can't tell
if I should fight or give up, no one
around to say, "You're enough."

Police Brutality

Abraham Jaramillo

Where is the man my mother fell in love with
where is the voice I never heard in a lullaby
where is the shield to protect me from the storms
where is the giant in the eyes of a child

Time goes by, and no sign

Where is the one to confiscate my phone
where is the impatient mechanic who
I should be handing tools to
where is the over expressive couch
where is the man kicked out of the game

Time goes by, and no sign

Where is the late night driver picking me up from work
where is the one to yell, "If you live under my roof..."
where is the teary-eyed grown man who can't stop me from
        moving out
where is the man telling me stories about his old man

Time goes by, and no sign of change...

Hands, Work, and Life (Life's Handwork)

Michelle Smith

The hand that rocks the cradle

is the one that rules the world.

Ageism, a silver tsunami in America

boons at 65+

AARP begins at 50+

Who will hold my baby boomer hands

gingerly

when someday the help I give today

may be what I need tomorrow.

As I hold their

multi-fingered and poly colored

make-up foundation

shaded appendages

wise and withered from the decades

or blessed to have reached 100 years old

These are the wonderful phalanges from nail to carpal

arthritic bones that crack and creek and open like a rusted window
sill in need of WD-40,

Waiting to be washed before a meal with a towel.

Hands are their windows clasped as one to hold,

a basket full of Jesus

because "He's Got the Whole World in His Hands".

Manicured and vintage nail color

or clear to see the thumbnail

of God's crescent moon

My hands have healed theirs

with pearl-colored, rose-infused lotion.

Bathed and massaged muscles from shoulder to the tailbone,

Snapped to jazz and bebop music and can still play the high
school brass band trombone,

Soothed their rheumatologic pains and knitting purl 1, purl 2 can
be complete

Shaked to meet and greet them warmly

Hands of wisdom, not of age

Hands that prepared Thanksgiving dinners and seasoned stuffing
with sage

Tell tales of experience,

and even turn a music book page

Their future generations rejoice in those hands that live in
their DNA

Morning, Noon, or Night

Ten fingers turn a page of life and

you will be amazed

even though not lightning fast,

They are stories indeed.

Hands

Luz Donis

I.

Small

held tightly

by all

to cross the street

Held a pencil right

to write

L-U-Z

Saved my face

when I fell

Picked a scab

till it bled

Resin stained

clutching a

favorite

tree branch

Where are you from?

What will you do?

II.

Youthful and anxious
leafing thru books
seeking a vocation

In training
dry and cracked
donning latex
powdered itchy
gloves

Filling paper
medicine cups
powerful pills
liquid concoctions

Skinny needles
piercing skin
threading red
rubber catheters

Sopping up
secretions
dressing up
wounds neatly

Wiping and tagging
newly arrived
wiping and tagging

newly departed

Where are you from?
What will you do?

III.
Experienced

giving back

reaching community

schools

supporting small

hands

Cold tired hands

on carpal tunnel wrists

managing care

distant untouched

care

Where are you from?

What else can you do?

Wrinkled

writing prose

Resting

folded

seeking

enlightenment

Night Shift

Tina Fallon

I find myself looking at the sky
Looking for something
a sort of sign
to show me what kind of night I might expect.

If it rains there is likely to be a chance of car accidents
Which means broken bones, a laceration or two
shatters of all sorts and
death, death is sure
to show up.

But on nights when the moon is full…
the spirits are loose and
things happen.

The drinkers, the overdosers, seem to pick that night to
do some damage

But on the best nights, hope smiles and lots of babies appear,
        sometimes with
their mothers, and sometimes
without.

Our hearts soon become so filled with
joy and love

that our bad memories are wiped

clean

because

with birth, a new

day is born

Silent Connector

Lois Jackson King

A long time it was, before, we became friends

Now our fellowship, I hope, will never end

You are a comforter, and bring joy to my life

Between you and myself, there is no strife

Many may say I could do much better

Because they think they are trendsetters

But I know the bonding, which keeps us

A true, hands-on connection with no fuss

You meet the needs that I ask you for

You give me that, and so much more

I don't have to get up, you do it all

Whatever the request, you're at my beck and call

Your response to my fingertips

You care so much, correction given when I slip

A great communicator you are, by far

Your great functionality, in my life, makes you a star

Not just a screen, keys, and monitor; you are my sidekick

A fully reliable and trusted computer, with every click

Envy

Michelle Smith

Envy colors my mind

And paints thoughts

of comparison.

It's bad-tasting medicine.

Poisonous venom in my veins.

Paralyzing into my tomorrow's brand new day.

Comparing who I am

And

What I am not.

I want to snap my boss like a tree twig

Break that strumpet in half

Honestly...

I value my freedom beyond the workday.

What a newsreel!

I cannot afford the

prison-bars-for-life-cost.

Jesus, take the wheel.

Placated I am my own mirror,

I am the captain

of my have and have nots.

I want to breathe fresh air and positivity.

Her 18 years vs my 1.5 years,

Ironically she even had the nerve to ask

Am I the age of 60.

I too serve a purpose in residential care:

Earned the angel wings of my CNA license

And possess

frequent flyer miles,

Unconditionally...

And have flown from the tarmac

From experience of

the lifelong loving journey of raising my autistic son,

So don't even go there.

However, I don't allow the professional and personal life to mix,

My tossed (and tasty) oil and vinegar salad

Is none of her business.

Envy go away

and never come back,

I'll file you

In the library catalog card section

Your energy I desire to lack.

April 2, Merciless

Mojdeh Amini

April 2, we're teenager with volcano of energy, burning curiosity
and ambition of changing the world and the news

The news of stump speeches at the university was flying fast over
the city; I was certain many from the school would be
there but I decided to go alone

Alone and for the first time I was there, felt lost and surrounded
among gazillions palm trees Gazillions palm trees were
cuddled in layers and layers of the spring winds

The spring winds climbed up to the sky and blew up the thicken
clouds and lights where were scattered as stoke the
smoke suspended in the air

The air rapidly waved the barrages sounds randomly and he
started hearing gun fired and screams of many

Many and he could make it through alive, but many other no
chance of going back home like Cyrus

Cyrus was faded away in the chaos of the machine guns and no
seen again years after years

Years after years, unexpectedly it was in the news "April 2 Merciless"
and was circulated on Facebook jumped and zoomed
off in my eyes

My eyes skipped many words and found Cyrus among flying
boundless gunshots into the air

The air held my breath and the skipped words began healing my
pain but the city remained unsteady and unrested

Sacrificio/Sacrifice

Sanjui Martinez

Suele saberse desconocido

Aminora con palabras dulces el posible dolor

Cabe mencionar que el "YO" no existe

Roba tiempo sin sentir culpabilidad

Independientemente de parentesco

Fiel a su tierno corazón

Incita una sonrisa que sana.

Coraza Indestructible, sostiene.

Imposible de penetrar

Obsequio divino seguro le llegará.

Seems like someone unknown

Allowing only a hint of pain

Can say that "I" does not exist

Robbing time without guilt

Independent of any blood relation

Faithful to his caring heart

Inviting a healing smile

Casing hard to destroy, holding

Eternal gifts for sure will come.

Pain, Compassion and Joy

Lois Jackson King

At first I thought it was going to be more pleasant and a delight

It gave a sense of worth and great purpose in this medical fight

I understand life has moments of many ups and downs

Through it all, I was determined to wear no frowns

With strong amount of compassion, I will meet the challenges

There were times when I thought, should I stay or should I go

The truth is many times my inner person was full of fear

Nightmares that rattled my mind, and jabbed as a spear

The sickness, the condition of many patients give me no ease

I feel their pain and their hurt; it's like the virus, attacking as
    it pleased

Some are gone, physically home, and the rest, spiritually at rest

I'm giving it my all and all; but yet, I don't feel it's enough

I acknowledge that all life does indeed matter

I acknowledge that all life is indeed precious

I am their strength in the time of their weakness

All my work comes from a place of love, inspired to do my best

I show no favoritism; I try to make every patient feel special

Rendering care, both spiritually and medically; I feel great

I have joy because I am able to provide care that is needed

I smile as I give my service of care; I "glow" when I speak of
    my career

Purity in uniform, everything was all white

Precious are the hands from God giving care without a fight

It's Harder to Go On

David Fallon

When your mother dies
A piece of you is gone

When your mother dies
You can't listen to her favorite songs

When your mother dies
It's harder to go on

I wrote a book for you
And it helped me fly

I wrote a book for you
And it let me let you lie

I wrote a book for you
But I still ask why

The days are shorter
Sunsets less sweet

The days are shorter
Making me want to retreat

The days are shorter
Feeling less complete

Time for moving on
Time for singing new songs

Time for writing
Time for righting wrongs

No time for losing more time
Time to move on

Today is a Day Of:

Mojdeh Amini

Sprinkling love over the broken hearts

Sprinkling light over the darkened minds

Sprinkling fairness over the taken knees

Sprinkling rains over the gloomy days

Sprinkling songs over the sorrowed souls

Whosoever will give its heart to love?

Whosoever will open its mind to change?

Whosoever will grieve to heal and forgive?

Whosoever will tear to smile and welcome?

Whosoever will give its words to write and sing?

Today is a day of

sprinkling love over the broken hearts

Whosoever will give its heart to love?

The Cackling Crow

Tina Fallon

I have a Cackling Crow
She is my familiar
But no one can see her
Only hear her

I have a Cackling Crow
She's somewhat of a Joker
A common manipulator
But mostly instigator

I have a Cackling Crow
All she wants to know
To make the tension grow,
She fancies a horror show

I have a Cackling Crow
She likes to be seen
Always high on caffeine
For us, no in between

I have a Cackling Crow
She loves to sing and mock
Enjoys her own squawk
Never lets you talk

I have a Cackling Crow

Guilty of comedization

Accessory to personification

A murderous association

Pets, Scruffy, Bunny

Karyn Grasse

People need you,
Evidently. We
Take care of you. You give us
Someone to love.

Scruffy little thing
Crawling under the newspapers
Rattling the cage
Under your sibling
Furry,
Fluffy
You bring us great joy.

Bringing joy, and
Unexpected surprises,
Nibbling
Noiselessly,
You make us happy.

Milo

David Fallon

Ellie finds three newborn kittens. Only one lives through the first night. For a few weeks, it is touch and go.

Hourly feedings. Gentle belly rubs to expel urine and feces. A visit to the vet to discover infection and dehydration. Treatments of intravenous fluids and antibiotics.

It takes a couple of months for the kitten to open his eyes. A few months more for him to walk straight and use the litter box. Eventually, he thrives.

Ellie names him Miracle because it's a miracle that he survives. She calls him Milo for short because she knows that people will roll their eyes at a name like Miracle.

Milo is unusual for a cat. He doesn't run from strangers. In fact, he runs to them with his tail pointed high in greeting. "He's a people cat," Ellie explains to astonished strangers.

Soon everyone in the neighborhood knows Milo. He makes regular visits to the houses on the block.

"I thought he was a stray," says the guy across the street.

"I didn't like cats until I met him," says the lady around the block.

One day, Ellie's nurse friend, Jean, comes over for some pizza and wine. Milo jumps on her lap and purrs. "This cat needs to be a therapy cat," smiles Jean as she scratches Milo's head.

"A what?" says Ellie in confusion.

Jean tells her about the animals that come once a week to the hospital where she works. How they cuddle with people who are sick. Or just lay with them for a while to keep them company. "It makes them feel so much better," Jean says thoughtfully.

The next week, Ellie sends away for a course on "How to Train a Therapy Cat." There isn't much to it. Can your cat stay on leash? Yes. Will he scratch or bite? Never. Is he okay in a carrier? He's fine. How is your cat with strangers? Excellent. It's not long before Milo is able to earn his certification.

On his first day, Ellie is more nervous than Milo. In fact, Milo is not nervous at all. He takes to it like a duck to water. He snuggles up to a little boy who has leukemia. He takes a nap with an elderly lady with dementia. He shares a tuna sandwich for lunch with a guy recovering from a diabetic stroke. When it's time to leave, everyone asks when Milo will be back.

Milo does this job for over 15 years, a long time in cat years. Then, one day when Ellie brings out the carrier to go to work, Milo tries to move. He is unable to get up. The vet diagnoses him with kidney failure. "Treatment will only slow it down," says the vet sadly. "But his pain will never stop." Ellie makes the agonizing decision to euthanize Milo.

When the vet leaves her alone with Milo to say goodbye, Ellie cannot stop crying. She apologizes over and over to him. She wraps her hands lovingly around his face and gives him tender kisses. Suddenly Milo purrs loudly and licks her hand as if to say that it's okay. "So long, my Miracle," Ellie says before calling the vet. It takes only moments after the injection for Milo to pass.

That night, Ellie feels more alone than she ever has in her life. She dreams. Dreams that her Mother and Father are still alive. Dreams that they have taken Milo to live with them so that she can go back to school. Dreams that she graduates to become a doctor. When she wakes, she looks for Milo. She cries again when she remembers he is gone.

Years later, Ellie finishes nursing school and gets a job working at a nursing home. The elderly patients love her because she is so attentive and caring. Then, one day the therapy animals are brought in. One of them is a cat. As soon as the carrier is open, the cat makes a beeline for Ellie. It will not stop dancing under her legs until she picks it up. The cat purrs softly and rubs its face against hers. Ellie tears up, remembering her Miracle.

"Maybe it's time?" she asks the friendly cat. The cat

mews in response.

Ellie makes a plan in her head to stop by the local animal shelter. At least to take a look.

To Mr. Charles Bukowski & The Bluebird

Mojdeh Amini

Your Bluebird is invited to my heart
A place to laughter and to weep

Your Bluebird is welcome to my thought
A place to sing and secret to keep

Shall the Bluebird to be and to beat in any hearts?
Let's go with him places to drink and to weep

Shall he sing and fly to Europe and anywhere else?
Let him not be a secret to keep

What Color is Your Bluebird?

Gustavo Reyes Ramirez

Everybody has a bluebird in their heart.

Yes! A bluebird, a la Charles Bukowski.

Everyone has a bluebird inside, trying to get out.

Tina's bluebird is a cackling crow, black as midnight.

David's bluebird wears a tux! It's a penguin, a symbol of survival.

Harper has a mockingbird, all the shades of gray.

Maya's bird was caged, and dreamed of being free one day.

Luz's bluebird lights up the sky.

Jerry has 2 phoenixes!– from the ashes they fly…

Luis has a Paloma–the symbol of peace (Pigeons can also fight
        till death)

Ms. Walker's bluebird is the color purple, and takes away
        your breath.

Me?

I have a Unicorn.

that flies like Pegasus.

My bluebird comes

    with pixie dust

            and flies in rainbow

Bluebird in a Cage

Anonymous

I am a bluebird in a cage,
A feudal tyrant cut off my tongue,
He is afraid
the people of the world know
the truth, because
he is illiterate, doesn't know
any words, can't read any words.
Not to mention
running the country.

I am a bluebird in a cage,
The foolish king wears his new clothes
every day, he thought he
would be respected
when he put on nice clothes,
Because he is an ignorant
tyrant, does not respect human
rights, does not protect minorities, he won't
have any friends, he didn't know
only a dictator in this world would be
a dictator's friend.

I am a bluebird in a cage,
The arrogant king cut me

and my fellow birds off,
He was afraid
other birds would know
of his atrocities, because he thought
to cut off all social ties, he will maintain
his power, he doesn't know
a regime that doesn't elect
and pass democracy
is a lie.

My bluebird is my weapon
against aggression
from outsiders.

One day, my bluebird that is
in a cage, will break free
from the cage, fly
to the free world.

Writer's Block II

Karyn Grasse

This will be a good day.

I am *so* ready to write

> —but first, of course, a cup of coffee.
> and, maybe I should get some snacks ready, just in case

> (I might get hungry.)

> and I should wash the dishes that are just sitting there
> before I do, I mean there are only two and it really won't
> take long at all.

> *Yes, snacks.*

> and I really have to clean up the office. I just can't think
> in an environment that is cluttered. It's distracting. My
> mind feels unclear. Hard to focus. I need an orderly
> environment to work efficiently. For the creative juices
> to flow unhindered.

> —I need to warm up this cup of coffee.

> I FORGOT TO FEED THE CAT!!!

Yes, I am so ready to write.

—But I should change into some comfortable clothes first. Something not so binding. In case I wind up working for long time.

If I'm going to change my clothes, I should REALLY take a shower first. I might not get another chance today.

notif I *really* get on a roll!

This might be my only opportunity.

Besides — I feel a little itchy.

Then I will be really primed to write.

Ah, nothing like a nice hot shower.

Snuggly, comfy clothes — Check!

SO ready to write!

But first, I think,

A NAP!

Pure Connection

Katherine Vega

I see you

I see you there on your bed

Working to take your next   b r e a t h

I   feel   you

I feel you shifting to a p o s i t i o n that isn't painful

I am connected to you

I am connected to you as your body feels just a *bit* better

Somos dos almas enredadas.

Y compartimos tu dolor, tu felicidad, tu sanación juntos.

Hasta el final......

I am empty

I miss you

I think of you

I hold you

I love you

Te Amo...

March on March

Mojdeh Amini

March 8 is here again and more relevant than ever, why?

Outspoken and shouting for so many overdue rights, again

Joining the remaining broken pieces of women everywhere

Dreaming of no "Women's Day" ever again

Equality the most wanted now, not tomorrow or the next year

Hands of many colors, clinching in again and marching on March

Angels of Love

Lois Jackson King

Oh my, to me, some come alone; giving loving care

Oh yes, and some, in loving groups, they do share

With bags of goodies, lots of prayer, and then some

With kind and sincere hearts they do serve

With a hearty smile and sweet hellos, a hand of praise they deserve

From the mission of God in their heart, they do not depart

With a made-up mind, their focus of duty they do chart

The thought of care directing the part, giving me a blessing

Not as in silver or gold, but the lesson of compassion

The love they gave, and I received, it cannot be told

A surety, it comes from a heart of love and can't be sold

In no way is it ever full of talk, but of satisfaction

Some may criticize, or stub their nose, but stop not their action

Their "hats" are many; and not recorded, so I can't tell

But with the blessings of God, their hands of care will never fail

What Happened?

Katherine Vega

I can't feel it
I can't feel the hate they say I am supposed to have
I can't feel the betrayal that we know took place
I can't feel the resentment of all the confusion in our relationship

Tell me why, Tell me why it had to be this way
Tell me why, Tell me why I wasn't allowed to trust you
Tell me why, Tell me why we had to battle so much
Tell me why, Tell my why we couldn't feel each other's love

You were magic to me when you would provide advice
You were magic to me when you would innovate to make ends meet
You were magic to me when you would make us laugh
You were magic to me when you wake us up and sing Las Mañanitas

I love you for being open to listen to me
I love you for being able to take a deep look within yourself
I love you for being a beautiful artist
I love you for all the love you provided to us

I am sorry I couldn't explain what was happening to me in my body
I am sorry I couldn't say what was bothering me
I am sorry I couldn't hug you when we were in pain
I am sorry I couldn't forgive you sooner

Please forgive me for being rebellious

Please forgive me for holding such harsh judgment

Please forgive me for being so afraid of you

Please forgive me for holding back my love

Thank you for being amazing here on earth

Thank you for making the decision to heal

Thank you for your commitment to ensure we succeeded

Thank you for sharing your brilliant mind

Ink or Pencil/Permanent or Temporary

Lois Jackson King

Your eyes once held the warmth of compassion, of love and care

They are revealing now the inner care of thoughts, of the silent mouth

Flowing loudly, ugly marks for all to view, is this truly the real you

The cutting words are piercing, like a sword

Every word full of bitterness, inner expressed anger, and
uncontrollable hate

Care once more, and purposed a turnabout to make a difference

Should we care if in our life there's a need for a change?

What say you, open that heart of care once again;

Wellness in words is the way

Resurrection from the inside out; show yourself

Sure and mighty; guided thoughts by a renewed spirit

Be molded and refined to the betterment of life for all mankind

Reveal once again bright and shiny eyes; full of care

That ray of light, which gleams even at night

Permanent way of brightness, which radiates hope, energizes
strength, gives life to dreams

Ode to the Working Ode

Michelle Smith

Pissy, pissy, pissy

Where have you been?

The way you walk sure nuff is a sin

As you are scratching the shiny brown floor,

 hurrying for your din-din

(Inhale, exhale, tiringly)

I smell the yellow river entering my nose

Inadvertently my goose-bumped skin's pores are open

 as if they were a water hose

And they need to be rinsed off by a water hose.

Am I a janitor too?

And here we go again.

Hissy, hissy, hissy

Where have you been

On "The Sadness of Black Folk in America"

Mojdeh Amini

As a newcomer to the Black American history, it may be fair enough to say that I am just not ready to write about the sadness of the Black Americans and the White Americans.

However, listening and participating in Dr. Cornel West's talk while analyzing the *Killer of Sheep* movie and reading his notes motivated me to get my head around it and step in to share some of my takeaways.

The Sadness of Black Americans

Mojdeh Amini

It's a kind of sadness that was born from inhumanity of man to man

It's a kind of sadness, that reborn everyday with the lights and darkness of days and nights

It's a kind of sadness that grows silently in scream of cruelty

It's a kind of sadness that rises with sunrise, but never ends with the sunset

It's a kind of sadness that penetrates humans' cell to cell and touches souls' scene to scene.

It's a kind of sadness that leaves scars behind in the presence of miracle touches

It's a kind of sadness that is justified by all the living gods in the sky and the ground

It's a kind of sadness that gives up hope and gains it again within the next breath

Monster-Slayer

Ani Minasian

Monsters be gone! I'm indebted to thee!

Once and again, you are rescuing me!

Not chiding my fear—if they scamper or crawl,

Squisher of demons—you conquer them all,

Thrashed with a broom or smashed with a walker!

Ever in action, you're no empty talker.

Rare though the case when your aim is mistaken,

Staunchly you'll charge into battle, unshaken

Leading the chase into dark corners deep,

All to imprison assassins of sleep.

You're still my dear champion, o ragged grey knight,

Easing me into a slumber each night

Rest will I under your keen watchful sight...

Sydnet

Lois Jackson King

(meaning: wide meadow; also spelled Sydnee; people with this name like to work; it's a religious name)

Sweet personality, as honey, from the honey bees

Yielding of yourself, oh so warm and tenderly

Doing your best; and always caring, as you should

Extra services you gave in my needed space

Night and day, every moment, ending with, love, as you begin

There is a loving heart beating high, above all the rest

What's the Point?

Luz Donis

Bestowing

Repeated visits

Obliged to do

What comes

Naturally and

Impulsively

Effecting a

Pointless

Offering

In your time of

Need

Tenuously

Standing by...

the life-sustaining process

Ayan Ortega

becoming a nurse is a process
and if i don't mind saying

i was brainwashed
to smile through the fatigue

in my body as much as my heart
it was only part

of the training, though it seems
the immune system itself

requires no such training

> t cell makes their rounds
> they, diligent
> its receptor locates the cells
> with virus hiding inside
> cytotoxic t cell receptor
> alerts its t cell, releasing the salve
> killing the cells
>
> they, without question,
> get to work.

metabolic break-time

the life-sustaining chemical reaction in organisms
i'm not allowed much time for this

the life-sustaining process: food
into energy for strength, growth

and breath in me, of me, and from me

as my five-year-old nephew plays piano
Does he know he is sustaining me, too?

motion to percussion
percussion into perception

perception to emotion
a tear
in, of and from me
the metabolic transfer

is a process, if i don't
mind saying

Acrostic Care

Tina Fallon

My mom is being cared for
I know she is well taken care of
she is the last parent I have
everyone in the house helps
rationale is out the door and un-
able to survive under the circumstance,
but there is
love
everywhere.

Hope

Lois Jackson King

Am I here and am I there; (estoy aquí) therefore I am everywhere

I can feel, but can I be felt, many heart breaking times

Beautiful sun shiny days; with much darkness of heart

What is the greatness of tearing the elements apart

Pardon me, I am here too; as close as any one thing can be

Room for all greatness; we will work together and fit to a "tee"

I can see stress and acknowledge the many uncertainties in life

Allow me to extend the right hand of a spiritual fellowship and "hope"

Hope is faith in what you believe to be true (lo que crees que
es verdad)

One God; One Faith; One Baptism; the "Hope" of new beginnings

A great feeling of being here; let's participate together as life builds

Newness and spiritual gain; we have always been within, seen
and unseen

It's now, time for change; pull from the deep, inner inspiration
and pride

Write it loud; our pen will be heard, will be seen somewhere
and somehow

So let us now begin fully equipped with all needs; and above all,
there is "Hope"

The Fall

Mauricio "Soul on Fire" Moreno

One fucked up thought, growing
into hate. One desire for love, gnarled
into tragedy. One mention of rebellion,
conjuring destiny you never wanted.

Your name erased
from Creation, your efforts
pulverized under a righteous fist, your pain
ignored by the Father. Instead,

your villainy, immortalized. Your name
a desecration, your actions judged
not as a whole, but for
the moment you questioned God.

You are a victim to a merciless
deity wearing His hypocrisy
like a warm aura
around His head, while you

must wear your horns
like a pillory for the world
to curse. Scapegoat
for the sins of an unforgiving

world. Slave to the freedom
you sought. But no one
bothers to ask you, Lucifer,
about your broken heart. Not even

a sliver of sympathy exists for
the villain of this narrative. No one
dares to question why God's
favorite angel was never afforded

the same forgiveness He promised
the Humans. No one cares
to wonder whether
or not Evil Incarnate ever

asked himself, "Where
did I go wrong?"

Grief

Michelle Smith

For Mom, Nana, Sister, Aunt, Great-grandma, Great-aunt,
Niece, Cousin, and Friend, Lady Gemini
June 8, 1937-June 29, 2020

Grief

Feelings deep enough to swim in

I'm sinking from the cries

Spinning in a hole I cannot crawl out of

The suffocation traps me

And the truth that you are gone

Cannot be denied

I am loving you

I am trapped

I am consumed

I am powerless

I am missing you

Grief

Is a thief

In heaven you are free

On Earth my heart is broken

And if all the pieces could form a ladder

and lead to you

I wish they could

A

Celebration

OF LIFE

BARBARA ANN SMITH

June 8, 1937 - June 29, 2020

I want and should

I wait and would

Float to the ancestral flight

There is comfort in knowing

You are in the best company of our family

Queen Mom and Matriarch

Shining Stars

And celebrities, writers, actors, politicians, and more

I wish they could

I wait and would

I want and should

It's not my time

"To be absent from the body is to be present with the Lord."

A red heart shaped "I Love You" birthday balloon

From you through Good messaged me so

Grief

Prepared me to know

Your being welcomed in God's Angels arms and wings

It ebbs and flows in waves

in seasons

nights and days

Is it true that time heals all wounds?

Collectively and separately

We will all grieve.

Don't Fall for Me

Luz Donis

You don't know me
You only think you do

You tell me I've changed
that we've grown apart

You don't know me
      only   you do

You   changed me
    we've grown

You   changed
   we   grow

You don't know me

I'm

trying to get   to know me

Trying to get
         to know

You do   know

        No   me
        No   you

To Be or Not to Go or Stay

Lois Jackson King

Let you out; is that all you can say

With your crazy thinking, you will soon fade

Do you need them, can they make your day

You are the source of my strength; don't you go away

I know all this has been said before

I must be strong to walk out the door

Make it quick and fast, or courage will hit the floor

Maybe a strong booster shot is what I need

The desire of my inner spirit is making the plea

Power thoughts fill my mind; saying you can and you will

Even when so many haters are not fully thrilled

Fear not and stand up; face challenges and stand out

Allow no more excuses to be found in you

Go ahead and do what it is you must do

Removing false shadows of past hurts and shame

Realizing the inside of you was the blame

Remember, the true you comes first, and fail not to forget

This makes way for very little or no regret

Once Again

Mojdeh Amini

Once again, an unleashed WAR is landing on
Ukraine to give up its heart, Kyiv

Rockets rolling recklessly with air raid sirens
fooling the wise and peaceful sky

As they are a crow of migrates winnowing,
like Wilson's Snipes ready to fight

Once again, the peace chapter tears apart
forcing the history repeated itself page by page

Once again, a caucus race shamefully acts,
throwing Ukrainians into a fierce wolves' WAR

Once again must fight to death for every inch, and crawl
many miles away from Kyiv, without facing back

As spring knocking millions of doors, sky asking skyscrapers
turn lights off to save migrating birds on the flyway home

Group Anaphora 2/8/22

Conchas y Café Bilingual Community Writing Workshop Participants

No time to say goodbye
No time for a last dance
No time to grieve
No time to find your resting place

I have no regrets, I leave you with peace
I have no regret to find you in a starless sky
I have no regrets, I've howled to the Moon
I have no regrets to have argued with you

It marches on as I stand by
It marches on to a place beyond
It marches with the countless unknown
It marches on, then I lost myself

It marches on, from hurt to pain
No time to say goodbye
I have no regrets, I leave you with peace

About the Authors
Sobre los autores

Mojdeh Amini

English is my second language, and from my childhood I have been fascinated by reading books from American writers such as Mark Twain, William Faulkner, and Ernest Hemingway.

Ayan Ortega

I am an artist and learner living in Compton, CA. Having worked primarily with visual art, I'm learning to be comfortable working on my sporadic writings in order to turn them into something meaningful to me, and maybe for you too.

Lois Jackson King

Artist of flavorful writings for every age level. A proud mother of 4, with 11 grandchildren, 11 great-grandchildren, and now 1 great-great-grandchild. Retired educator, minister of the gospel and love for humanity.

Gustavo Reyes Ramirez

Gustavo R. Ramirez is a poet-teacher-student-activist. My mission is to co-create a world of peace, love, dignity, laughter and well-being through leading by example and acting now. I will live life to the fullest with courage, integrity, bold action, adventure and fun!

Michelle Smith

Michelle Smith is a poet and artist working toward producing work that emits love and empathy for people of all kinds.

Tina Fallon

Tina Fallon has contributed to *Conchas y Café* since 2015 and has published, *The Bin... and Other Pieces of Trash* in October of 2020. She has a BA in Theatre from Cal Poly Pomona and several courses in Elementary Education and Child Development. She loves avocados, piñas and tv!

Kathy Vega

Kathy Vega is an LA native now living in Atlanta. She is grateful for the experience to be a writer with DSTL Arts via Conchas y Café. She feels that through the stories of her ancestors, humanity can continue to evolve and progress towards love and understanding.

Sanjuanita (Sanjui) Martinez

Sanjui works as a teacher at LAUSD. She has four adult kids, and lives with two of them and her dog Oreo. She enjoys reading and writing.

Rocio Diaz

Rocio Diaz is a first-generation undocumented mujer who graduated from Cal State Los Angeles with a BA in Theatre. She is a Mexicana poet, writer, producer, advocate, artivist, and future lawyer in the making.

Abraham Jaramillo

Abraham Jaramillo is a multimedia artist; illustrator, graphic designer, and photographer. His love for the arts began back when he created small sketch galleries for his grandmother when he was 8 years old. A longtime volunteer and teaching artist with DSTL Arts, Abraham enjoys and nurtures the pursuit of knowledge both in himself and others.

Karyn Grasse

Karyn is a Monterey Park native and has been writing short stories and poems since she was 12. Sometimes, they get published. Sometimes, they sit in a box. Her most treasured creative endeavor, however, is the charming little person who has invaded her life for the past several years.

Jing (Heidi) Wu

She/her. My book is on Amazon: https://reurl.cc/Wk4YZL. Podcast: https://reurl.cc/nEVbjD

Nikolai Garcia

Nikolai Garcia grew up in South Central Los Angeles and currently lives in Compton. His first chapbook was published by DSTL Arts in 2019. He sometimes makes friends on social media: @hellokommie

Ani Gohar Minasian

A descendant of Armenian immigrants and survivors of the Armenian genocide, Ani Minasian is an LA-based writer exploring themes related to tolerance, ethnic history and cultural preservation, self-empowerment, and her own struggle for artistic expression. She has written plays, songs, poetry and short prose in Armenian and English, often blending languages to create bilingual works, and is currently working on her first novel.

Luz Donis

A second-generation Guatemalan and second-generation L.A. County Nurse. Born in Chi-town raised in Boyle Heights. I've had the privilege of working, volunteering, and serving my community. It's been a joy finding my Spanish, English and Spanglish voice and expressing it through the Conchas y Café Zine.

David Fallon

David Fallon has published short fiction, articles, poems, and plays in various publications and with various publishers, including DSTL Arts. He has a collection of short stories entitled *Longing for the Moon* which is also published by DSTL Arts.

Mauricio Moreno (Soul on Fire)

Mauricio Moreno is a 1st-generation Colombian-American artist and writer, originally from Elizabeth, New Jersey. He moved to California to fulfill his life mission of being a writer and sharing the stories of others to bring readers closer together and heal the world.

About the Conchas y Café program

Conchas y Café is a 12-week workshop series for adults, focusing exclusively on creative writing, literacy, and illustration. Participants have the opportunity to work with volunteer writers and artists on developing artwork that will be published and presented in a triannual 'zine and public reading.

For more information, locations, and dates for upcoming Conchas y Café workshops, contact us by email at *info@DSTLArts.org*.

Acerca el programa Conchas y Café

Conchas y Café es un taller de 12 semanas para adultos, especializando en escritura, literatura, y dibujo. Participantes tienen la oportunidad de trabajar con escritores y artistas voluntarios en el desarrollo de obras de arte que serán publicados y presentados en publicaciones trimestrales y lecturas públicas.

Para más información, localidades, y fechas de próximos talleres de Conchas y Café, contáctenos por correo electronico al *info@DSTLArts.org*.

This program is supported in part by:

This publication was produced by DSTL Arts.

DSTL Arts is a nonprofit arts mentorship organization that inspires, teaches, and hires emerging artists from underserved communities.

To learn more about DSTL Arts, visit online at:
DSTLArts.org
 @DSTLArts